# I AM ONE OF YOU

NICOLE M. K. EIDEN

Mississippi Sound Publishing, LLC

Copyright ©2016 Nicole M.K. Eiden

All rights reserved. Except for brief quotations in critical articles or reviews, no part of this book may be reproduced in any manner without prior written consent of the publisher:

 Mississippi Sound Publishing, LLC
1822 23rd Avenue
Gulfport, MS 39501
www.mssoundpub.com

ISBN: 978-0-9882126-5-7
eISBN: 978-0-9882126-6-4
First Edition

Library of Congress Control Number: 201591097

Author photo by Jennifer Potts

Cover and interior design by Hope King

Titling set in Avenir Next

Poetry set in Palatino

# *dedication*

I dedicate this book to Mary Irene (Mitchell) Eiden, Beatrice Elizabeth (Caton) Johnson, Jane Ann (Johnson) Eiden and all the creative women who came before me. Especially to each one who has never called herself an artist but has always made the choice to heed the hum around her and create something with care. Making dinner, making celebrations, making costumes, making hard days better.

The cover photograph was a gift from my Grandma (Beatrice) Johnson. She is the smart gal on the bottom left. When I evacuated from New Orleans in the hours before Hurricane Katrina, I took this photo with me as my most valued possession.

Grandma Johnson didn't leave behind many uncompleted projects. She figured out how to go to college. She taught school. We crunched jicama from the garden and played Double Solitaire. She illuminated the sewing machine and demonstrated how to be fervent for basketball, yelling when a foul isn't called. She showed me how to ask for help.

Even now, years after Grandma Johnson has gone on, her spirit is busy in my mother. I pick up the phone at midday to call my mom, to ask her what she's working on – whether it's mentoring new teachers, making my daughter's Christmas stocking, or coming up with another good solution. But primarily I call because I want to hear her voice and feel how she listens, just like her mother, my grandma, did.

On my other side, Grandma (Mary) Eiden wrote poetry. She loved listening to classical music in the living room after dinner.

If you followed her into that room, you had to pay attention to the music. She would make and freeze individual meatloaf suppers to last the month. After my Grandpa died and she had a little money for the first time in her life, she bought me a video camera. She knew I wanted to be a filmmaker. She wanted to help me tell stories.

When I was older and would visit, I remember the mound of sewing projects layered high in a cabinet, material bought on sale during the 1970s oil crisis mixed in with newer embroidery kits and yarn. But her heavy life got in the way and the majority of these undertakings would go undone.

I still feel a prick of sadness when I think of the many projects that she left unfinished, but with more reflection, I now recognize her hope.

No matter what was lacking (money, time, support), Grandma Eiden held it in her mind that she could make something beautiful. That was work.

While many plans went unrealized because of the unceasing tasks on the ever-present "to do list," what has been made, what all these women have brought into being, is where my eye will always go.

Each of these women showed me how to create a consequential life.

# I AM ONE OF YOU

# I AM ONE OF YOU

| | |
|---|---|
| Real Mohicans don't dress for the weather, at least not on Halloween | 1 |
| Air arrives in a suitcase | 3 |
| My Blank White Bumper Sticker | 4 |
| Daily Life | 7 |
| The Bridge | 8 |
| Mortgage * | 10 |
| Longer Time | 12 |
| Spoon Rest | 13 |
| Watch me gather, watch me drop | 14 |
| When I'm With You | 15 |
| It's never just a speck | 16 |
| My hands are awake | 18 |
| The nest in the tree balanced out the window makes | 19 |
| To Know the Smell of Ohio | 20 |
| Moving back to New Orleans: the same poems move me every time | 21 |
| To My Child, For My Parents | 22 |
| Not how I want to die | 24 |

| | |
|---|---|
| Sitting With a Yardstick | 25 |
| Driving Home | 26 |
| What Is Today | 27 |
| After receiving a letter from Elwyn who is already putting on her winter woollies | 28 |
| Loneliness made me walk back | 29 |
| I love you can't stay inside my body | 31 |
| Reason Enough | 32 |
| Prayer | 33 |
| Harmonica | 34 |
| The Name We Call Letter | 35 |
| If Words Were Primary | 36 |
| Work With Centrifugal Force | 37 |
| Everything in This World | 38 |
| *acknowledgments* | 49 |
| *about the author* | 51 |
| *praise for* **I Am One of You** | 53 |

\* 2016 Women's National Book Association Writing Contest, 3rd Place

# Real Mohicans don't dress for the weather, at least not on Halloween

Finally big enough almost cool enough
to wear Kathryn's real deal Indian princess costume from last year
Grandma makes me pull on navy tights, school shoes, my bright
green wool sweater. I grump, cannot argue. Reach down to tie
plain shoelaces, protest inside. She doesn't get it,
Kathryn wore real moccasins with forest ready soles.
Mom would know the costume comes first, Dad
would recite directly from *Hiawatha*.

Grandma takes me back to my neighborhood,
but this time to Kathryn's yellow house.
Two doors down, my house stands unmoved.
The grass is mowed. The light is on.
It is the old country before the war.

Kathryn and I prowl our blocks for packs of candy corn
the inevitable popcorn ball. We trade loot, save
the best. Our favorite tree, our climbing rock
all look bewitching in the Halloween night.
I forget the malice of these inaccurate tights. It is effortless
to be with my friend again.

Dragging pillowcases now heavy with candy, we come full circle.
I stand in the driveway of my closest friend,
face to face with my house once more, it hums
warm in the pre-winter night.
Without warning, the overwhelming urge to pee
to relieve, to go home surges through me.

It is my house, I run to it
bang on the side door. Mom must be dozing
Dad is in the basement on the computer. Or changing laundry.
I must be in my room petting my cat.
No one answers    my bladder on the verge    this is my house

someone must come. Tears come.
I miss my dad. My mom.
Beat the door.
Kathryn pulls me into her
house to use the bathroom there.

Later, Grandma picks me up
I am crying. She covers me
with the green afghan that is always
in the car. The road leads back to her sweet ordered home.
I know where everything is.

Grandma draws a bath to close
this cold October night. I soak.
I know my parents aren't home.
They are in Seattle getting a bone marrow transplant.
Facts are facts and I am not a conjurer.
I pull the plug. Water disappears down.
Dry off with my special towel, Grandma's rose powder.
Grandma tucks me in, the twin bed secure.
Holds my hand, we pray
for Mom, for Dad.
She reminds me that the felted banner I made
for his birthday hangs radiant in his hospital room.

Grandma turns out the light.
One journey behind us.

## Air arrives in a suitcase

morning unpacks elephant fog early
                inside my house only

floorboards that point toward coffee are aware of me

I creak open the wide window
        shoulder echoes wood's careful word

                fog steps inside
                      an autumn morning inside my bedroom

scooting back, the cushions of my chair know

        work can wait
        faucet can drip without flood
        laundry was born to sit
        dust knows the meaning of longer

it is alright I say
        to have unfolded open drawers of clothes

yes, I see crushed wool sneaking out
some days it is
        raw itchy me trying to escape

but not today
there are letters in my head to write
        I have things to tell you

I close hands around my letters, my cup
        and all air that is not yet day

## My Blank White Bumper Sticker

still on my car now I like leaving things
        the way they happen
        rain seeped through plastic
                smeared the words blank

you need age to arrive
you cannot just create
        a diner in 2012
            paint it shine to reflect the sun and everything else
              expect the street to believe it is
                    sixty years old

detail
I feared lockjaw
        the randomness of things
a brush with rusty screw on the see-saw
fatal mouth peanut butter freeze up
detail
when I was eight my hair was straight
I turned thirteen
agitating hair looped
                    up in my blind spot
                now tighter after tighter
                  curl in motion tells
            every woman at the Xerox store my state
                  constantly searching for a pen
detail
I played on the Dodgers
red shirt t-ball
shortstop between

      pinpoint positions of second
                              third make a note
detail
when I'm asked to be there at 7
I say 7
        think sehven, I'll arrive
                I can't say my alarm clock is accurate

I've been compared to it
        measure last minutes before being where
                            with elastic
                                    stretch around
                all the time you need to get there
                (preferably with your hair combed)
detail
I wonder about
the electrical lineman I met
                in the nursing home
how he felt supplying
energy all over Morgan County
                        for its very first time
from those poles his
delicate fingers touched electricity

lights glowed from each house
he surveyed his work from one hundred feet up

detail
(the Nile River is 4,258 miles long)

       who measures
       the longest river in the world?

       with what do they measure?

       the length a shadow casts
                       across the lawn divide
                       or multiply by \_\_\_
                            arrive at
                            height of building

I want to hold the wrinkle of my hand
look back years and remember the shovel

I want to be the pole
run currents directly to the skillet

I want to be a hammer and pound
make noise see where my energy goes

A blacksmith has the horseshoes
to prove his work.

# Daily Life

A man outside Cesky Krumlov 7am
the railroad station      my eye gooping with infection

A man with a small dog walking
between concrete and old communism

I stand here
asking all history, all families
about continuing

# The Bridge

In the morning darkness
everything turns elemental
sock and shoe

a gulp of yesterday's coffee to survive
the hardest part, the
not feeling like myself

pushing through to get
past the empty road, I find
not the quiet I

try to cultivate, but
the definitive quiet
all around

there is nothing
but the wheel, my hand, this coffee and
one, two, three, brown pelicans looking

for food, searching like me
in this open space
the birds nudge me to move

beyond this savage morning, over this
immeasurable bridge is
what is delicate, is what enters

when urgency falls away here's
my grandmother, her cabinet full
of dates bought on sale
here's my grandma, drawing curtains on a
pulley, tucking me into darkness
here's my friend's red-headed baby

all have gone before me
it's a growing list like
a mission, this quiet bridge

those I've loved deeply
those I've loved as much as I could

I will see you up ahead

# Mortgage

This house that we built is lovely
Here, I sleep next to you every night

Remember when we were unfamiliar. I had a plump life
you had a plump life

we were busy with our things
we tried to be loved by other people

Remember that messy life

But then, as they say, we got together
we had sex every day

Who knew when I would ask the wrong question
The instant you would turn dull

But you weren't scared of scrambled eggs
You were keen to walk the dog

And now here we are every night

It's after midnight, sapped from balancing plates, people all night for cash
Exhausted from nailing floorboards and keeping hair off the tub

My calves ache and I don't want to give
It's the end of the month is there enough for the mortgage

I want to buy a hardback atlas, the book that split
the Germanys, took me to the USSR

pressed my kindergarten watercolors proved
my humble town existed

The atlas is $80
But we need toothpaste
I want to see a movie – can't, can't, there's not enough
it's the end of the month

I move away from you. Find your own dinner.
Do you want something or are you just hugging me good night?

The 1st comes – we pay the mortgage, another month
You reach out again. Your hand says Come here

All weighty words fall second to the comfort we create
I don't wonder what you want. I quickly kiss you hard.

## Longer Time

Walking home across those memory syllables
                                      I repeat over again
all around everyone, it is almost sundown
                the kind that doesn't occur too loudly

I pass the bridge where my father and I stood
                            spiraling likenesses of each other
      sometimes I smile like a man who has lived fifty years

My body looks over this small town and can not decide what month it is
        striped scarf rolls long below my feet
                      it must be sometime after true cold sets in
     late January

Nothing seems to matter but my walking steps,
                      light shadow creasing
     I squeeze out every knot in three, save-worthy tears

Something speaks below this plane of muscle,
                  speaks directly to the person I won't admit I am
      hear this in moments when all that lasts in shredded pocket is
          no desire
              when no song is

      but the song of wild toes coming through my soles
all the motions day and I have ever contended with split apart
                                grey, hinting orange

# Spoon Rest

There's something about
the soft roundness
of the dish that
catches the spoon on the stove
that makes me angry
it is there to help a
crook who steals
soup right from the pot

I've seen how this
stove saver coddles
tells spoon "alright alright rest yourself
in me"     she doesn't care about all
the stirring spoon has done
inside black iron kettles
she doesn't give mind to spoon's
crosshatched scratches
evidence that spoon has knocked
ham shanks against slick hot vats

The fact that
spoon could stir chili or
Hungarian noodles all the same
she doesn't even address the issue.

# Watch me gather, watch me drop

Standing on the cliff whirling
blackberries down
through the clouds
voices of human stain into
my far off basket
a hundred pies potential
the local bear silently
swaggers and steals
I am left somewhere
here standing on this rock
with a pair of dripping purple hands

# When I'm With You

I want to have a basket on
my bike too    find

every hole in the street
avoid falling and celebrate

such fortune

## It's never just a speck

It is 65 degrees Fahrenheit
There's a speck of spinach
on my freezer door

A speck of green that made me question
who made dinner here
in my kitchen who tore

leaves without my consent
and left
slipshod mess

I sit back Yoko style
it is evening
schlepping from page to page

always eyeing that speck

across the room
I toss down
my book

doodle without
a pen on the counter
wondering about the speck

you and the dinner I didn't attend

there's that nickel speck
hardened spinach
I pick at
ooze down

I squat, following you
and your dinner
juice dripping to the floor

I throw the speck of you
and melted orange popsicle (for added liquid)
into crooning blender
frappe faster
lid loosens

everything inside flies out
my kitchen
perpetually moving
away from me
the woman who peeled carrots here first

liquid river mess
I cannot follow with rag
quick enough so
I cover up my seeping muck

I mean no one ever
notices a speck of spinach when
you offer a quince

# My hands are awake

I am coffee mulling
over my short fingernails
and the way I share
love for breakfast
your chair floats always
around the table and I am
sitting on the waves of a guitar

Why was I created with so much
morning begins a chance to filter
down to the neglected
where I can figure what fills
my porcelain mug
your cup handles caffeine, breath
heart stop and I
must raise my
strength flooding from
the thickest reserve

# The nest in the tree balanced out the window makes

me feel everything I've lost, my sneeze
remains too long at the end of my short nose
all my bones ask my belly

how do you give yourself away
to individual people, rock to dust disappearing
who pack up all you are in their own carry on bag
chuck it from any plane

the nest perched middle high this morning of possible rain
the nest is confidence that the wind is
not too strong, that a future exists with food

I sit under wool blanket, wondering
where all this love energy goes knowing
I have hands that hold large bundles
I have legs strong enough to shore my arms and what they carry

sit on this morning of potential rain asking all
nothing counting no birds
but seeing pictures
all that is out of me with you and gone.

# To Know the Smell of Ohio

You don't have to
walk in the country
just step where
the river meets mud

Unlocked leafy smell
my childhood has passed
unlocked leafy smell
my friends have children

# Moving back to New Orleans:
# the same poems move me every time

I sit on a cardboard box in another new place, my in-laws' unspoiled
white house four days before the anniversary of Katrina

there is little blood flow in my body, I haven't said much
trying to be realistic, haven't seen friends

don't know what I expect from myself now back in New Orleans
pull out poems, washed out copies of copies

I sink down in the box, my tightening thighs know that I am
crying
sure it is hurricane loss, disarray

but mostly it is the poems, the immediacy of the lines
the way they wedged into me on the first read in college

alone, blinds pummeling out morning light
parallels how they move me now

afternoon, married, loving, loved

# To My Child, For My Parents

I look around my tender room and
think of all the things
I want you, my child, to know
of me, of life
poetry art kindness

But then, I can't help but want an easier
passage for you
Can't you love science more than your mother?
Won't you ask the questions
rewarded with money?

Tonight alone in my house
I cry the way blessed people do
I think of my parents guiding me
One foot in front of foot
You can do it artist,
you can make your world

In my thirty-six years, I have made much
friends, pain, discoveries, films
a marriage a home

Now we have created you
with love, touch, biology
Tucked under skin
In a world so deep, I feel I should know it better
you are stretching me out
you are pushing us forward
When I scrub,
When I laugh,
When I write
Even as your father's bow combs
the strings of his violin

My mother my father welcome me up
into parenthood
I pray I can usher you through
as they ushered me

Guiding one foot in front
Go create artist
I see you working. Look at what you've made.

## Not how I want to die

surrounded by piles
books
laundry Wednesday's
yellow sock
articles clipped

                  a long string from
                  my tenth grade jacket
                  I keep it for possibility
                  I might sometime need to

        extend kite in field
        all around me
        piles of what I was
        the postcard on my desk
        kazoo under chair

                in each new room
                I pick up
                notebook set by
                door grab

                        letters  by bed
                        slide over table
                        top piles reshape

        my stamped second grade
        thumb print emerges
        its seven year old size
        I take my hand now
        move up my same dry knuckle

                        fingers with deeper ridges
                        palm that stretches across more
                        piles stack they fall and
                        I haven't yet completed

# Sitting With a Yardstick

I measure things
        how many minutes
are left of this
        first hour after oatmeal
how many flat days until
        Wednesday at 3
how many nickels on the carpet
        saved for five o'clock coffee
how many hours looking for
        glove in my pocket

I stretch every
        rulered thought across
ironing board to press
        meter its worth
I clunk away scared
        every time I measure
scoot farther away from
        me dragging an ankle full of calculations

even in my sleep
        I portion out what I do divide
up my time between work
        not watering my fig tree errands
inviting hopefully coming
        people for dinner a week from Thursday

I have two and a half leeks
in crisper to cut finely sliced
for then

# Driving Home

head even
        in low atmosphere

eyes tall as half
        moon rising

I fall out of the car
        stunned by grace

## What Is Today

I don't want to admit that it is grey as board or
white as blank I sit
question mark body in my chair

so what
I planned to walk with you and your new dog

here at my house in my chair pouting
nothing to do
brain asks every corner of room

what action moves clearer than this
music    tea    book    dry noodle
to be boiled
separate for soup

# After receiving a letter from Elwyn who is already putting on her winter woollies

*For my daughter's namesake*

in France, you have weather too and you
must have a coat by now

in New Orleans, here, not a cold leaf in
sight only my cat's continuous paw this

calendar says
 I have known you one year it is
October again

# Loneliness made me walk back

towards the house
looking for a pen this pen

to write about the walk or not
walk I was walking, list begins

two robins swimming, encircling each other
dialogue proceeds, "the rain has stopped,"
other robin sings, "I'm clean, free"

freedom: when the muscle between two
shoulders loses sight of

worry becomes wing
pulling curtain away

outside the window
not dry after hours of rain

it is human to want
April air not by yourself any longer

it is human to walk into
door with finger in own eye

to pull carrot out by the hair
forget it in drawer to rot while you grouse of (fill in)

to go miles in distance
but short depth inside

the rock how we become quiet
rock with holes

not lacking
but indentation

distinctive fossils
sculptures of where we come from

are and are going the rope in a circle
how scary to use the word God

# I love you can't stay inside my body

I have said words to an Italian
words that slipped out between other words and no words

maybe I wanted a promise
hands around me still

when I came back to America
but maybe I love you is

all I know to care about
in Ohio, some days

I regret having a
mouth that speaks like
the organ it is

# Reason Enough

All morning stretched
grey rain through
missing leaves sweet

Song around trees
getting wet nested flying
sweet song

Single drop
           slides to collect

I am dry
I am good

# Prayer

You've heard that even
playing baseball is prayer

opening a jar for a child or
child opening door for you

is gift
two people who love each other

maybe unevenly, maybe not enough
can we ever articulate where we

fit together how far we will go in
I can only go on answering yes

Some have done it before us
the street outside never hears us walking

only me
passing with dog

the green house finally asks your name
can I really say

love or I love you or
I think you somewhere down
love me

there are no short cuts
I remain open-handed

# Harmonica

earthwork crayoned
in sundown hush

patent of my heart

# The Name We Call Letter

        as in character as in
a or c even
        d which ends thud
the name we call letter

makes word
        friend word
who joins like chains or
        curtains floor to ceiling making
room where we live
        a man enters a waiting room

parlor is
        where a man waits for a woman
waits for a precious someone
        who each time is a particular someone
who holds particular things inside

her pocket something
        a word is waiting
to extract our sense of balance
        or imbalance onto
page into space of air
        from throats starting

as letter
which doesn't know anything about
what I do on any given day

# If Words Were Primary

then why would I have
eyebrows that arch up your
back to your head rolling
between ears and lips

eyebrows that like to kiss your legs touch
all your hair

# Work With Centrifugal Force

if the middle is stone

bash your head clutch your arm pull
your bloody heart behind you in a net

drag it through the street at noon sleep with it
when no one answers

when you know this net this heart
this bloody trail the stone crumbles you glide away
a horse through long grass

# Everything in This World

1    Not long after Adelaide was born, intensifying after Corey died
Claudia couldn't drive. Not in the city.

The winding country roads, like the one near Old Man's Cave
where I, seventeen, laughing in the backseat
spun sharply, one stick from ravine's edge
                      the closest I have ever been to death.

Those roads are still
doable. It's the rushing lanes, compacted space
that spark anxiety.

Over the phone, we talk about my trip home.
Between bits of conversation, we piece together
the elaborate plan. Her coming up
by way of the in-laws, her child
staying with them, me
driving us down to
Cincinnati, triangle around the state.

No one asking the world,
just hours, miles. Giving up breakfast with
another singular
friend in town for a beat.

This favor so easily done, such an innate part
of friendship, that I am baffled by this fresh
                      certainty rising in me.
Driving Claudia is the most vital thing. Meeting her need gives
confidence in the world. My daughter hops over me and laughs.

2  We wave goodbye to Adelaide, to Elwyn
   get rolling in my parents' car.
   Without husbands, daughters, nothing
   to pay attention to but the road, each other.

   The seat belt digs roughly into my neck.
   Claudia reaches over, slides the mechanism down
   to better placement. The adjustment takes,
   we continue our exchange.
   How much home improvement remains
   how our children learn, we curve into the limbs of our religion
   how having no money wears you out
   all the ways we order the chaos.

3  We arrive at the hotel room we are sharing
   with friends. Jason opens the door, boundless hug.
   He has warned us
   a bottle of Voignier is chilling.
   Jenny fresh from the shower,
   in a melon crepe dress is already sweating badly.
   We discuss options.
   We all agree
   she would be more comfortable
   in the sleeveless olive shift.

   A knock. Tara and Amy bust through,
   two more of our band. We trickle down
   to the lobby, a gathering up.
   We hug, pick on each other. Remember when you said that.
   Feels good to reach back and feel the people we were.

But even more, we talk about now
tiny things, the best gin, new shoes.
In the cab, I am surprised
my shyest friend is taking public speaking classes.
I am not surprised
Amy is finally going to run for office.


4   We have made this same journey
    for each one of us, starting
    eighteen years ago, Heidi and Joe.
    So many weddings
    church, park, field, hall
    jazz and now
    here we are
    back in Ohio.

    Each wedding unrepeatable
    Each wedding welcoming in
    someone new: field guide, architect, inventory manager
    my husband, a violinist, and in late August, a cop
    don't ask to wear her hat.


5   Today, the longest day of summer, extends for Megan and Izzy.
    From up front, the officiant pronounces, "The beginning."
                    common wedding code, we are hungry
    Continues on to middle
                    sun crushing hard, will there be champagne?
    I squint, adjust my legs.
    "World without end." We know these words,
    the years at Catholic school.

Megan, Izzy hand each ring to the other.
Next to me, Claudia leans forward, doing her best
as witness.

Megan beaming. Izzy,
radiant on the pulse of moment.
The sun no longer a fight.

These two standing in front, the rest of us
spiraling out
hair combed, shirts tucked, dresses,
mixed in with sisters, cousins.
This place, once merely words on heavy paper
a day, an address.
We have made it here on time.

Over and over we go our separate ways
arrive together again and again.
This world without end.

6   The ceremony does end. There is champagne.
We determine which bar has the short line.

Pull together chairs, delight in hearing good stories.
How is Owen already seventeen? Thunderstruck,
someone says, "In a band, at a bar?"

The circle widens, small portraits emerge
Success at work, adoption, a third baby.

We have come this far together not
because of joy, nor history. A harder list:

Because at seventeen, surrounded by softball players,
too many beers in the afternoon, we could call
Come pick me up. I'm not telling you yet, I'm gay.

We have come this far because at twenty-nine
baritone, Johnny Cash, surprise I can sing.

We have come this far because at twenty, we bombed
out of college
pulled each other to the other side of town,
ransacked the best thrift store.

We wrote letters
opened letters
parked right outside Uncle Sam's Pawn Shop
heart still smoldering from
lightning heartbreak
bought tambourine.

We have come this far because now,
we are the artist with arthritis
coursing each finger joint.
Because at twenty-one, we awoke from
coma without arm
drove left-handed across the plains to be together.
In the face of divorce, we arranged flowers, became a doctor.

We have angry parents, aging parents,
We've withstood the wrecking of a city.
On the worst night, we have flown to be side by side
when a child has died, when a brother has died.
Stood at funerals of mom, dad.

We will not experience everything in this world.
But if we are dedicated to others, we go through it all.

7  All pictures have been taken.
The last song comes.
Despite pressure from Jenny
the DJ never plays what she is waiting for.
It would have been good.
We pile into the cab, ramble back
for one more drink
or two. Just below the surface of celebration
is baby Corey.

A week after his memorial,
we converged on Claudia and Andy
Broccoli salad, fizzy water, egg salad.
Around a table in the country sun, we grieved
even laughed, we are funny when we are together,
our families all look different now.


8  The next morning, Claudia and I rise earlier.
We tap Jenny and Jason out the door
bye dear friends. We don't wake anyone else
the road leads East.

Yesterday's conversation thickens.
We are quieter, tired, I say
How, just because you
have a kid, can you stop trying
to do what you are trying to do?

How can you say
I have been raised by
parents, you are being raised
and you will someday raise?
This is all there is, kid, this is all there is.

Unquestionably, the child is most essential.
She must be loved, helped through school,
shown the necessity of kindness.
I want to run the road beside her, more than anything.
I am a mother, run ragged but I am on fire.

A desire shoulders up to me,
impels me to uncover

what it means to
be part of something, not just repeat, make oatmeal
buy the next size shoe

to see myself past
my skill set or lack of
past all this muscle I've created
all these years of hard work.

To really go at the heart of the day again and again.

Can't all this inclination to take care of someone else,
foster growth, forge art
live hand in hand
Can't the mystery of life contain all these rigors
There must be room for what I am trying so hard to make.


9   It is late, I ascend the carpeted stairs
    my childhood home, I am thirty-seven.

    Pause on the landing, face family pictures
    antique wedding portraits, my grandmother, Mary Mitchell,
    too poor for a wedding dress.
    I never knew how striking she once was until this picture,
    her best wool suit, her life ahead.
    My other grandma, Beatrice Caton,

an artful veil trimmed in lace.
Mine patterned after hers.

My own parents, no formal wedding portrait.
It was the seventies, they say.
Once, I grouped loose snapshots from a shoebox.
Mom in dotted Swiss, Dad made a matching tie.

Finally, a picture of Mike and me on our wedding day.
My dad in the wrong suit, my mom, beautiful, unworried.
The rain has passed, the light is what we all hope for.
We have stood at the altar, looked out at those who
know us best.

The last portrait, the one that doesn't always
grab my eye, my great-grandma. She is stern,
the photo, soft as a pencil drawing.
I know my own grandma, freshly married, cared
for this woman, her new mother-in-law, until she died.
This was the story passed down.
This is what we do.

What did they talk about, cool wash
cloth after washcloth. I know my grandma was listening
to her new husband's dying mother.

And the rest I know as legend.
My grandparents moved to Ohio.
Grandma didn't unpack
for a year, sure they would return
to upstate New York. One day, she opened
a box of linens. Had two more children and
Ohio became home.

Not quite a fact: Mom met Dad met
at an anti-war Catholic club.
Did Dad leave mom with
dishes on their first date? The narrative remains unclear.

I hurdle to my parents driving me down to
Louisiana. I know they are shaking their heads,
this is not comfortable. Too deep, too South.
But I find Mike in Louisiana. We all know that I cannot meet
Mike in any other state. And now we are parents,
we have Elwyn.
The passing of time is
not just state miles, hours, or the carrying of genes.
It is in the words that we hear, repeat.
Words Elwyn, the great-great granddaughter, will one day say.

## 10

Three more stairs above this landing,
my parents in their room, behind the other door
my child asleep, in her crib, my childhood room.

Claudia says it is our job to be examples
I see the way I am going

I've sensed for many years, under words
I will never be elderly

My friends, our children,
All these family portraits, tell me something else
I am one of you.

# *acknowledgments*

Loudest thanks and deepest love to my husband, Michael Harvey, for his soundness of mind as we make our life together. Unending gratitude to my parents, Jane and Gregg Eiden, for their support and vision. Much credit to the tiny but powerful group of writers that helped me stack words into something better than before: Chet Nicholson, Eden Labouisse and Constance Adler. I am thankful for the writers who have made time for my work all along, Robert Kinsley and Jill Allyn Rosser. Thanks to Amy Turn-Sharp and Amanda Page, writers who catch what I throw. Thank you for the encouragement to keep coming to the writing table, Elizabeth Pearce, Allison Alsup and Beth Bingham; I never tire of toasting these three. Gratitude to Jennifer Potts for always capturing the image through her camera. Thank you to creatives Andy Cook and Brad Richard for their attention to detail. Thanks to Michel Varisco for friendship and mentorship. For helping me read the small print, thanks to Dale Brinkman. Much love to my gang from C-bus. It is a privilege to be part of our enduring friendship.

Lastly, immense gratitude to Kristen Necaise and Gail Nicholson of Mississippi Sound Publishing for carrying my words farther than I could have alone.

## *about the author*

Nicole M.K. Eiden is a poet and award-winning filmmaker whose work captures the simple challenges and beauty of ordinary life. Nicole hails from Columbus, Ohio. She arrived in New Orleans in 1999 and never looked back. Nicole holds a Master of Fine Arts degree from the University of New Orleans and a Bachelor of Communications degree in video production from Ohio University in Athens, Ohio. Nicole co-owns Windowsill Pies, a Southern-style pie and tart company in New Orleans.

The author (above) and her Grandma Johnson (left)

# *praise for* I Am One of You

"… this skillfully written collection … is sure to be appreciated by anyone who enjoys contemporary poetry."

**BLUEINK REVIEW**

"… In James Baldwin's 1956 novel *Giovanni's Room*, a character muses that "perhaps home is not a place but simply an irrevocable condition." If Eiden's poetry is about any one thing, it is that irrevocable condition. It's about the old home we leave without ever quite leaving it, and the new home we build out of some uneven mixture of coincidence and desire. It's also about marriage – the unlikely effort to forge a home with another human – and about children, and our hopeful wish to strengthen a home for those who come after us … On this tour of all her homes, the poet writes with pride but without arrogance, with wit but without guile, and with grace but without unnecessary ornament. Moving poetry that kindly welcomes readers in to sit down and rest awhile."

**KIRKUS REVIEWS**
**Volume LXXXIV, No. 5, I March 2016, page 149**

"Nicole Eiden's poems arise from a profound desire to find something crucial – something durable and palpably significant – in the quotidian moments that compose the greater part of our lives. Her poems range from musings on a speck of spinach on the freezer door, to sweeping, lyrical meditations on time and desire. She can shift tone on a dime while delving into the murky ways in which we not only seek to define ourselves as parent, worker, friend, spouse, citizen, son or daughter – but also to break free of those definitions. These poems are acutely aware that we are all moving on the currents of a river whose source and strength derives from our collective and personal histories, but that we must look ahead, push forward, embrace the future as well. This is a delightful debut."

**J. ALLYN ROSSER**
Author of *Mimi's Trapeze*, *Foiled Again*, *Misery Prefigured*, and *Bright Moves*

"The author writes her way through the world so gently that you are not expecting tiny punches to your gut. Air sucked in by lines that simply appear and make you move your face in ways you had forgotten. *"We tried to be loved by other people."* Her poetry always makes me feel like I can nod my head and announce to the rest of the room and the world that we are all the same. We are moving through things in this life. We are traveling with her."

**AMY TURN SHARP**
Author of *Hold Me Like Ohio*

"These poems explore a common life, offering cadences of the everyday in images of school shoes, a small dog, a cup of coffee, a child, a mother, a father, a husband, a wife, while moving in memory's landscape from Ohio to New Orleans and points in between. But these are not just simple moments, but rather moments lovingly attended to, lovingly attuned to what it means to see the world in both its joys and sorrows and to not be afraid. These are incantations to turn to when the path seems dark. Trust me, they will help."

**ROBERT KINSLEY**
Author of *Field Stones* and *Endangered Species*

www.ingramcontent.com/pod-product-compliance
Lightning Source LLC
Chambersburg PA
CBHW031215090426
42736CB00009B/928